God's Chosen Angel

And

The Special Arrival

by Penny Tronzo

illustrated by Tom Gibb

Cherubic Press
Johnstown, PA

Published by

> Cherubic Press
> P.O. Box 5036
> Johnstown, PA 15904

To order additional copies send $8.95 plus $2.00 shipping and handling to the publisher, above.

First Printing January 1997

Text © 1996 by Penny Tronzo
Illustrations © 1996 by Tom Gibb

ISBN 0-9646576-1-9

Library of Congress Catalog Card Number 96-85585

All rights reserved. No part of this book may be reproduced in any form or by an electronic or mechanical means without written permission from the publisher. Reviewers may quote brief passages to be printed in magazines or newspapers; distributors / retailers may use quotes from this book as promotional material.

This book features a vinyl laminated cover providing sturdy protection for your child's book while saving natural resources.

Printed in the United States of America

*Dedicated to
Our Heavenly Father
and our Lord Jesus Christ*

with forever love to my son, Chad,

and my dad (Grandpa Jack).

*Special thanks to my family
and friends for all their support
and love and to Jean LaCoe for
encouragement.*

Heaven is a wonderful place, filled with everything a little boy could dream of having. The little angel loves to play baseball with all of the greats - - Roberto, Mickey, and Babe. God watches over the little angel and all of his friends because he loves each and every one of them; and because that's what God does best.

"Come on, Little Angel!" yells Roberto. "This ball's for you!"

"Next time you might hit a homerun!"

Back on earth, a very lonely and sad man and woman pray to God for a child to care for and love. God watches them from heaven and carefully listens to the prayer.

"Dear God, we would love to have a family.
If you could find it in your heart to lend us one of your children
we would be eternally grateful."

God hears their prayers and pauses. He looks around at all of his beautiful angel children. God decides the little angel would be the perfect son for the lonely man and woman on earth.

> "Little angel, I have a very special mission for you.
> I'm sending you to earth to live with a man and woman
> who would love to have a son just like you," God told him.

"But Heavenly Daddy," said the little angel, "I'm not sure I want to go. I like it here with you and all of my friends." The little angel looks very scared and starts to cry. All of his angel friends look sad because they know they will have to be apart from their little buddy for a while.

> "Don't worry," God says. "You'll be back someday and all of
> your friends in heaven will be waiting for you. I'll always be
> your Heavenly Daddy, but for now your mission is to bring love
> and joy to a man and woman on earth who need you very much.

The little angel thought about God's request for a moment.

"Okay, Heavenly Daddy," he said. "Just as long as I can come back to you someday."

God smiled and wrapped His arms around the little angel and wiped every tear away. He then whispered,

> "You are my very special little angel, and I love you very much, but now you have a special mission."

The little angel smiled and happily ran to tell his friends of God's special mission for him.

God looks down and is pleased with His miracle which is growing inside the mother. He quietly whispers,

> "You will give birth to a very special child. He is a gift from me. Love him as much as you can for as long as you can, but remember, he is mine."

Finally the day arrives. The little angel is carried from God's arms to the mommy and daddy. God is very pleased and holds the three of them tightly in His arms as He gently whispers,

"You can borrow him for a little while, but remember, he's mine."

The mommy and daddy love their baby with all of their hearts and decide to name him "Chad."

Chad grows up quickly, trying all sorts of new things. He loves his mommy and daddy very much, and they love him too, but his friends in heaven are always watching over him. Chad is fulfilling God's mission by loving and bringing joy to his earthly family and friends. God is very happy to see His children enjoying life and each other and knows that Chad loves Him, too.

God also feels pain when His children are sad or hurt. And just like mommy and daddy who take care of Chad when he gets hurt, God and his angels are always watching over him, too.

Mommy and daddy hold tight to every moment with Chad. They have a wonderful time together, and they are very grateful that God has blessed them with Chad.

Chad grows and grows, becoming smarter and more handsome every day. He and his parents are very happy. But God misses His son and wants him back in heaven to live with Him. God gently whispers to mommy and daddy,

"Enjoy each moment with Chad, but remember, he belongs to me."

Chad is becoming a young man and God is allowing him to experience all the wonders and pleasures life has to offer. God wants His son to continue to bring joy and happiness to many people. God wraps His arms around Chad and his new love and gently whispers,

"Dear Chad, fall in love and have a wonderful time, but remember that you are my son; you are my beloved. You will soon be coming home."

"Chad," God said. "I miss you very much and it's time for you to come home to me."

Chad was upset. He didn't want to leave his mom and dad and all of his friends. "But Heavenly Daddy, I love my mom and dad. I don't want to leave here. Can't they come, too?" Chad asked.

"No, Chad." God answered. They'll be coming soon, but they need time to learn how special they are to me."

Chad thought about God's request, and he knew he must trust God's wishes. Even so, he was very sad to leave his parents. "Okay, Heavenly Daddy. My place is in heaven with you," Chad said. "I'm ready to come home." God was happy and gave Chad a big hug.

Though Chad wasn't sure he wanted to go back to heaven, he was glad once he got back. He had forgotten what a wonderful place it was and couldn't wait until his parents, family and friends joined him. He was so happy to be home again, back with his Heavenly Daddy, home with all the people in heaven who loved him; happy to wait to embrace his earthly mother and father and brothers and sisters.

After Chad was gone from earth, his mom and dad were very sad for a long, long time. They knew that God loved them very much, and they prayed each night that God would hold Chad in His arms and give him a kiss from them. They also knew that some day they would see Chad again when they go home to heaven. They were so grateful that God had chosen them to love Chad for a while. For they had cherished and enjoyed him on earth, and they knew they would all live together, happy forever, in heaven.

And once in a while, on clear, dark nights, they can see Chad's homerun balls zoom across the sky.

Gently they hear Chad whisper, "Mom and dad, this one's for you."

(Part Two)

The Special Arrival

by Penny Tronzo

illustrated by Tom Gibb

Heaven is the absolute greatest, Chad thought.

When God had told him he had to leave his home on Earth, that it was time to learn just how deeply he was loved and could love, he felt sad but he knew his Heavenly Daddy knew best.

"Yeah, my life on Earth was good, but this, this is perfect!" he said as he looked around his heavenly home.

It is so wonderful that time goes so fast in Heaven. While he missed those he left on Earth, Chad was busy having fun and learning how to love his family in a new way; from Heaven.

God had already taught him so many things. He understood the many heavenly missions to Earth and what many of the missions were. And he understood why things happened there the way they did.

Chad watched closely as God worked His miracles on Earth and saw how the angels all cherished and cared for people on Earth.

Chad asked, "Heavenly Daddy, when can I watch over somebody?"

God smiled and said, "Someday soon, Chad."

Things seem different in heaven today, Chad thought. Everyone is so busy. "Hey, guys, how about some ball?" Chad asked his heavenly friends.

"Not right now, Chad," everyone answered. "We have to get ready for a special arrival, and we need your help."

"How, who, when," Chad asked God excitedly. "Come on, Heavenly Daddy! Tell me!"

"Okay, Chad," God said gently. "The special arrival is your grandpa Jack. His time on Earth is almost over."

God showed Chad his grandpa Jack on Earth. "Wow!" Chad said sadly. "He looks so sick and so tired. Heavenly Daddy, please do something!" Chad cried.

>God smiled lovingly and said, "Very soon, Chad. But first we have to get everything ready for him. And you have a very special mission."

"Me?" asked Chad very surprised. "I haven't been back here in heaven that long. Do you think I'm ready?"

>God hugged Chad. "My dear son, you're ready. Now hurry and get your stuff."

25

Chad took another look at Earth and at his earthly family. They were so sad. They knew they had to give up Grandpa Jack. His mission on Earth was finished. Chad felt sad knowing that his earthly family would be broken hearted and lonely again - - they way they were when Chad left them. But he also knew that time passes very fast and that they would all be together again in their heavenly home with God; happy forever.

Chad knew he could spend no more time watching what was happening on earth because there were so many things to be done before Grandpa Jack's arrival.

"Chad, it's time." God said. "Do you have everything ready?"

"I think so," Chad replied. "Help me review the list. I have a new white gown that will fit Grandpa Jack perfectly, the shiny gold halo, and the puffy white wings. Did I forget anything?"

God laughed and winked at Chad. "Yes, my son, you did. What is something you remember that your Grandpa Jack enjoyed very much on Earth?"

Chad thought hard and then said, "Oh, yeah! I need his favorite hat. He loved his hat." They both laughed.

God gently whispered into Grandpa Jack's ear,

> "My dear son, it's time to come home. Open your eyes and see what I have to give to you."

Slowly Jack opened his eyes. He was amazed. He no longer felt sick, no longer tired. He looked around in awe at the beauty he saw and the love that he felt. He looked farther and saw the most magnificent sight he could have ever imagined. There, standing in front of him, was our Heavenly Father, holding the hand of his beloved grandson, Chad.

> "Oh, Grandpa Jack. Welcome home!" said Chad and God.

As Grandpa Jack got onto the beautiful, white motorcycle that would take him to his eternal home, Chad talked nonstop. "Oh, Grandpa Jack! We are going to have so much fun! Heavenly Daddy will teach you so much. You'll understand how important your mission on Earth was, and how deeply you are loved and can love . . . and why sometimes people on Earth are sick and sad."

"God and I can teach you how to hit a homerun that looks like a shooting star to everyone on Earth and how to save a little bird from falling out of its nest. You can learn how God wipes away tears from sad people and heals their broken hearts."

"Oh, Chad! I missed you so much!" said Grandpa Jack.

"I know." Chad replied. "And Grandma and everyone down on Earth are so sad you had to leave them. But now you know we are all only away from each other for a little while. When God says "It's time," in just the blink of an eye, we'll be together again."

Grandpa Jack had forgotten how much he loved heaven before he went to Earth. All his heavenly friends were waiting for him to come back. They all laughed and hugged each other. Chad gave him his favorite hat.

Things were almost perfect.

"We have one special thing to complete now, God said.

"What?" asked Chad and Grandpa Jack. Gently, God, Chad and Grandpa Jack put their arms around Grandma. God whispered to them,

"Look up at the sky, My children." as He painted the most magnificent rainbow ever.

"We are with you all of the time," whispered Grandpa Jack and Chad as they leaned close to Grandma. "You will see us soon."